INDIAN GODS
AND MYTHS

INDIAN GODS
AND MYTHS

CHARTWELL
BOOKS, INC.

Published by Chartwell Books
A Division of Book Sales Inc.
114 Northfield Avenue
Edison, New Jersey 08837
USA

ISBN 0-7858-1079-X

This book is produced by
Quantum Books Ltd
6 Blundell Street
London N7 9BH

Project Manager: Rebecca Kingsley
Project Editor: Judith Millidge
Designer: Wayne Humphries

The material in this publication previously appeared in
All India, The Atlas of Languages,
Oriental Mythology

QUMIG&M
Set in Times
Reproduced in Singapore by Eray Scan
Printed in Singapore by Star Standard Industries (Pte) Ltd

CONTENTS

THE ROOTS
OF RELIGION

The Indian Subcontinent is a land of numerous tribes and languages, and the religions of the region are rich with complex mythologies that are both sophisticated and full of contradictions. Although eight out of ten Indians are Hindus, India is the home of many followers of other great world religions, including Islam and Christianity. Nothing, however, compares with the power of the ancient tales, handed down from generation to generation.

India is geographically diverse, with the great Himalayan mountains in the north, rice- and wheat-growing plains, desert and tropical jungle, high, tea-growing plateaux and low-lying coastal areas with palm trees, where the land is crisscrossed with waterways. The climate is extreme, the hot season brought to an abrupt end by the heavy monsoon rains.

Above: Kharding Monastery, near Keylong in Lahoul, with its elaborate figures of Buddha and bodhisattvas.

Opposite: This seated figure from one of the Buddhist cave temples at Ajanta is a reminder of the exceptional craftsmanship of the monks who lived in these temples.

Right: Detail from the Hall of a Hundred Pillars Temple near Kanchipuram, in southern India.

Below: The spires of Jaisalmeer's Jain temples were built between the 12th and 15th centuries, and were dedicated to Rikhabdevji and Sambhavanthji.

evil, exploring ways of living life and of facing death. They find these stories everywhere, in books and movies, theater and dance, sculpture and paintings.

HINDUISM

Hinduism developed from the Aryan or Vedic beliefs dating from around 2500 B.C., but by about 500 B.C. Hindu gods had become more important. The Vedic gods, like many of the deities of early belief systems, were animistic: personifications of aspects of the weather, like storms, wind, or fire. As the Hindu culture slowly overwhelmed that of the earlier Aryan people, the Vedic gods were assimilated into less important positions in the pantheon, still respected by the Hindus but accorded less significance. The gods of Hinduism were at once human and superhuman, and there was a feeling of warmth and even familiarity toward them. The greatest lesson of the epics is the final triumph of a kind of cosmic justice or balance.

REINCARNATION

One of the most important stages in the evolution of Hinduism was the concept of reincarnation — the belief that after death we are reborn to live another life. This belief is reflected in the Hindu view of the world in which everything is created, flourishes, decays, and then dies, only to be recreated in an eternal cycle. The supreme god, Vishnu, has three aspects: Brahma, the creator; Vishnu, the preserver of life on Earth; and Shiva, the destroyer.

Reincarnation and the cycles of nature are recurring themes throughout all Hindu mythology. There is always a moral to the story: how to be the perfect wife or husband, how to be reborn as a better person, how to behave toward others, how to keep the gods

LIVING FAITHS

In India, the legends and myths still seem so alive in the daily existence of ordinary people that they are, indeed, a part of life itself. Every fall, on the night of the great festival of Diwali, millions of tiny oil lamps are lit as dusk falls. They shine out, row upon row of them, from rooftops and window sills. Children settle down around their mothers or grandmothers to hear the story of Lakshmi, the fickle goddess of wealth and good fortune. Hearing this tale, and countless others, at their mother's knee, is their entertainment. They are absorbed in a rich fantasy world of gods and demons, princes and princesses, friendly animals, and exciting adventures. Their psyches have free range over ideas of good and happy with sacrifice and celebration. Much of Indian mythology holds a religious context, which speaks in particular to those holy men and women, priests, hermits, and wandering ascetics who are searching for the key to the ultimate nature of reality, and for the way to escape the endless cycle of rebirth.

For the historian, the language and images of the ancient mythological texts presents the ancient history of India. The migrations of the Aryan peoples into India can be followed by tracing the burial and cremation practices of the region, as described in the ancient Vedic hymns. The cultural influences of the

Below: The friezes at Khajuraho Temple are typical of many Hindu shrines, showing that the religion encompasses every facet of human life.

indigenous Dravidian peoples can be seen in the increased importance of the goddesses in subsequent sacred texts. The struggles of rival dynasties are vividly described in the great battles of the mythical epic poems, the *Ramayana* (dating from *c*. 300 B.C.), and the *Mahabharata*. The *Bhagavad Gita,* composed in *c*. 200 B.C., is part of the *Mahabharata*, and it was at about this time that the sacred Hindu texts, the *Upanishads*, were also written. From about 400 A.D., the *Purana* became the most important Hindu texts, with their accounts of the myths of the gods and the creation, destruction, and recreation of the universe.

Most of the stories in this book are Hindu tales, but other religions have not been overlooked. The story of the life of the Buddha, for example, is included. Although he is a historical figure, his life itself has been turned into an elaborate myth involving gods and demons, even though the Buddhist doctrine is atheistic. The Buddha is even sometimes described as an incarnation of Vishnu.

JAINISM

In the Indian Hindu tradition, the lives of famous holy men, saints, and the founders of other great religions are elaborated in similar ways. For instance, Mahavira, the founder of Jainism, was born in the 6th century B.C. after his mother had a visionary dream. The astrologers forecast his coming and the gods closely observed his young life, which was full of heroic feats.

Jainism emerged as a direct reaction against the elitism of the Hindu caste system and the Hindu tradition of sacrificing animals. Jains

Left: A painting of a highly detailed scene from the great epic poem the Ramayana, *one of the sacred Hindu texts.*

believe that the cosmos, or *loka,* has not been created by any one entity, but is eternal: it always has, and always will, exist. Jains, like Buddhists, do not believe in a creator god. Jain belief shares some Hindu characteristics, such as the search for *moksha,* the release from rebirth, and many of the same myths.

Salvation lies in conquering material existence by adhering to a strict ascetic discipline, which for lay people embraces special vows, or *anuvaratas,* imposing vegetarianism and not working in any area that involves the destruction of life (e.g., hunting or fishing).

SIKHISM

Traditional biographers also elaborated on the life of the founder of Sikhism, Guru Nanak, who lived from 1469 to 1539. Although he believed in only the one God, his birth was said to be witnessed by millions of gods who foretold his future as a great man. This greatness is exhibited in various feats of magic. For example, when his disciple Mardana was hungry, Guru Nanak turned poisonous berries into edible fruits. The story of his enlightenment is that he disappeared while bathing in the river and was presumed dead. After three days he returned and explained that he had been with God. His first words on his return were said to be "There is neither Hindu or Muslim, so whose path shall I follow? I will follow God's path. God is neither Hindu nor Muslim, and the path I follow is God's." But even in the *Adi Granth,* or "Original Collection of the Hymns of the Gurus," the one God is sometimes described with reference to the Hindu deities: "He, the One, is Himself

Right: This Buddha of the Indu-Hellenic style has a purity of line and form typical of the Gandhara school in Taxila, c.500 B.C.

Brahma, Vishnu, and Shiva."

Sikhs live disciplined lives, adhering to the five "Ks": *Kesh* – uncut hair, representing God's will; *Kangha* – the comb, symbolizing controlled spirituality; *Kirpan* – the steel dagger, or a determination to defend the truth; *Kara* – the steel bracelet worn on the wrist to express unity with God and adherence to the Guru; and *Kachh* – an undergarment representing moral strength.

Temples are a vital part of the Sikh religion, as Sikhs believe that God manifests himself within them. The "Holy of Holies," the Golden Temple at Amritsar, is the center of the Sikh religion and is thus the main site of pilgrimage in Sikhism.

SPIRIT OF THE BUDDHA

Buddhism originated in India, but spread to the countries of southeast Asia where it has become a major religious and cultural force. Buddhist thought shares with Hinduism its cosmological vision of time, including the transmigration of souls.

Gautama Buddha was born in northern India in the 6th century B.C., and the story of his life has become a legend which illustrates the main precepts of Buddhist thought.

QUEEN MAYA'S DREAM

The spirit of the Buddha appeared to Queen Maya of Kapilavastu in a dream: an elephant floating on a rain cloud, a symbol of fertility, circled around her three times and then entered her womb. Astrologers forecast that Queen Maya would have a son who would leave the palace to become a holy man. When

Left: This 11th-century sculpture of the Jain saint Parsvanartha expresses the austerity of the Jain doctrine with its simple line.

the baby was born, a lotus sprang from the place where he first touched the ground. Fearing that the young Prince Siddhartha would leave as had been prophesied, the king surrounded him with luxury. At 16 he was married to the Princess Yasodhara, and 12 years later their only child, Rahula, was born.

At about this time Siddhartha's curiosity about the outside world was aroused, and he ventured outside the palace grounds. Outside, he encountered for the first time old age, sickness, and death, and for the first time became aware of suffering. He also met a wandering ascetic and resolved to leave his home and become a recluse. After six years of extreme asceticism he realized that he was no nearer enlightenment than he had been while living in luxury, and he resolved to follow a middle way to enlightenment, free from desire.

THE ROAD TO NIRVANA
While meditating, Siddhartha was tested by the demon Mara, first with fear and then with pleasure, but he was untouched. Eventually he achieved insight into all his former existences, and achieved enlightenment while sitting under the Bodhi tree. He became aware of how the terrible suffering that wastes human life is caused, and how it can be eliminated by recognizing the four noble truths that became the basis of his teaching: that suffering exists; that it depends on certain conditions; that these conditions can be removed; and that the way to remove these conditions is to practise the eight-fold path – right views, right resolve, right speech, right conduct, right livelihood, right effort, right mindfulness, and right

Right: A Jain saint in the arms of his mother. This is an 11th-century stone icon from western India.

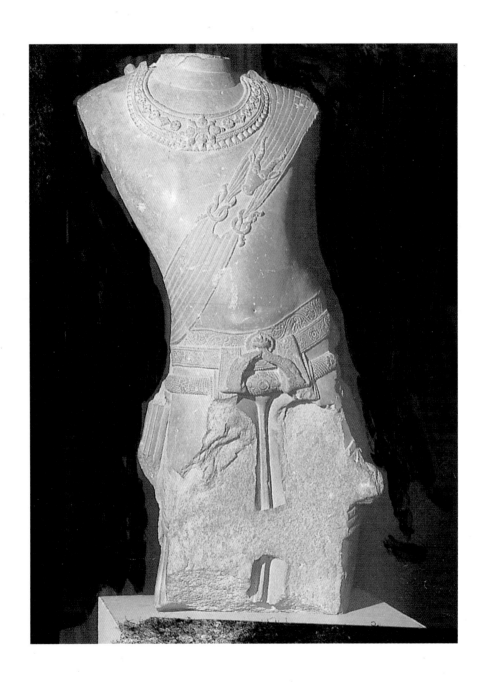

concentration. From now on, he was known as Buddha, a word which literally means "the awoken one." Forty-nine days later he set in motion the "wheel of teaching" by preaching his first sermon in the deer park at Sarnath. His deep sense of compassion and desire to communicate his ideas to others induced him to preach for the next 45 years, the remainder of his life.

BUDDHIST TEXTS AND MYTHS
The teachings of the Buddha are highly revered, but there is no single collection of texts constituting a "Bible" as such. Different areas of Buddhism produced their own manuscripts and collections of teachings.

The animal stories of the Buddhist *Jataka* use all kinds of folk tales to illustrate Buddhist values. Many have been floating around the world for centuries and turn up in different forms in Homer, Boccaccio, and Chaucer. (Some students of Indian mythology believe that Hinduism claimed the epic poems of the *Ramayana* and the *Mahabharata* in the same

Far left: The "Sanci torso," a red sandstone torso of a bodhisattva from Sanci, from the Gupta period, 5th to 9th centuries.

Left: Stone relief representation of the great stupa at Amaravati in Andhra Pradesh (now destroyed) from its own casing, c. 150 to 200 A.D. Buddhist stupas developed from burial mounds containing relics of the Buddha, to vast representations of the cosmos and centers of Buddhist worship during the period of the Mauryan dynasty (c. 322 to 185 B.C.), when Buddhism was the imperial religion. This stupa was exported with Buddhism, and in China evolved into the tiered-tower pagoda.

15

Above: Stone relief illustrating the Vassantara Jataka tale. In this story about one of Buddha's previous incarnations, he was Prince Vessantara, seen here giving his chariot to a Brahmin beggar.

way by inserting sacred texts, such as the *Bhagavad Gita*, at appropriate points in the story). "Each myth celebrates the belief that the universe is boundlessly various, that everything occurs simultaneously, that all possibilities may exist without excluding each other" (Wendy O'Flaherty, *The Origins of Evil in Indian Mythology*).

SCULPTURE

The most tangible legacies of Buddhism are the great statues that proliferate across India and southeast Asia.

Religion in India, and especially Buddhism, stirred the imagination of its followers and inspired them to produce amazing works of art, developing an artistic tradition that influenced the evolution of art throughout south-east Asia, China, Japan, and Korea.

Highly polished monumental sculpture began to appear in the 4th to 3rd centuries B.C., during India's first unified empire, the Maurayan. At the same time, Buddhists began erecting their dome-shaped stupas and to carve temples out of rock. Emperor Ashoka, a Buddhist convert, erected Buddhist monuments and columns inscribed with Buddhist edicts throughout his empire during the 2nd century B.C. His lion capital from Sarnath still serves as the emblem of modern India.

The Gupta empire, which flourished between the 4th and 6th centuries A.D., generated flamboyant, vibrant carvings, during a period of sustained magnificence. They diverged slightly from Hindu and Buddhist traditions into an especially Indian form.

CREATION
MYTHS

Hinduism embraces a very complex mythology, so it is not surprising that some of its creation myths are very abstract, struggling with the concepts of existence and nonexistence. Others are more concrete, and include the golden egg, or *hiranyagarbha*, from which the world is hatched, and in some the gods actively work to create the world. Some myths recount Hindu history, focusing on stories about drought and flood, the two great natural disasters most feared by dwellers of the Subcontinent for centuries.

Previous page: Impression of a Steatite seal showing a humped Brahmani bull, from the Indus Valley, c. 2500 to 2000 B.C.

Below: Putusa, the thousand-headed cosmic person standing on Vishnu. A 17th-century Nepali painting (gouache on cloth).

The *Rig Veda* asks a number of imponderable questions about the origins of Heaven and Earth, and none more so than "Did creation form itself, or was there something which pre-existed?" Originally used as hymns of praise during ritual sacrifices, the various creation myths of the *Rig Veda* help worshipers to focus on the reasons for their own existence.

ADITI

Aditi, or "the birth of the gods," propounds one version of the creation, whereby Prajapati, the Lord of Prayer, fans the gods into existence from nothing. A female principal already exists, crouching over the cosmos ready to give birth to the Earth and sky. Creation myths are full of paradoxes and cases of incest, and in this case the mother goddess Aditi and her father Daksa, the Sun god, are born to each other. The Adityas, the eight celestial Suns, emerge from Aditi into the primeval sea. Seven of them build the world, but the eighth, Martanda, is still-born, and his corpse is thrown out of the orb of the Sun by Aditi.

In this extract from the hymn of creation from the *Rig Veda*, the heavens and Earth emerge from nothing: "Neither not-being nor being was there at that time; there was no air-filled space, nor was there the sky which is beyond it. What enveloped all? And where?

Under whose protection? What was the unfathomable deep water? . . . Upon it rose up, in the beginning, desire, which was the mind's first seed. Having sought in their hearts, the wise ones discovered, through deliberation, the bond of being and nonbeing . . . Whereupon this creation has issued, whether he has made it or whether he has not – he who is the superintendent of this world in the highest Heaven – he alone knows, or, perhaps, even he does not know."

IN THE BEGINNING. . .

There are other stories in which the gods actively create the world. Prajapati, for example, rose from the primordial waters weeping because he was lonely and did not know why he had been born. The tears that fell into the water became the Earth, and the tears that he wiped away became the sky and the air. Then he created people and spirits, night and day, the seasons and finally, death.

In a creation myth using the concept of the egg (also found in Chinese and many other mythologies), Brahma is the creator. The golden egg grew from a seed which floated on the cosmic ocean for a year and shone with the luster of the Sun. Brahma emerged from the egg and split himself into two people, one male and one female, the incestuous union of those two being the creative force. Brahma is also called Narayana ("he who came from the waters"), who is described as lying on a banyan

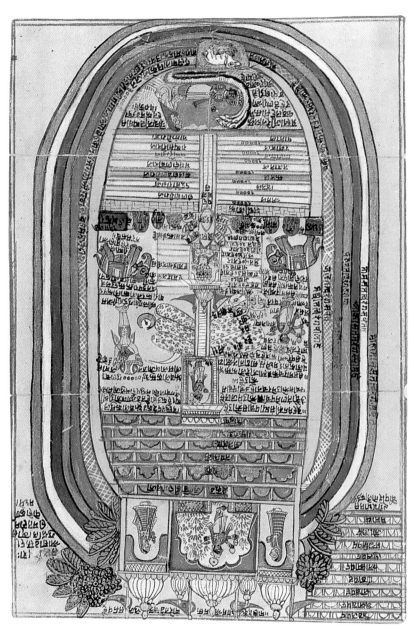

Right: The cosmic egg, according to Hindu belief; an 18th-century painting from Rajasthan. At the bottom Vishnu is reclining on the cosmic serpent. From his navel protrudes the lotus upon which sits Brahma. At the top is Vaikuntha, or the paradise where Krishna dwells.

Above: Many of the scenes on the stunning Kailasa Temple wall reliefs depict excerpts from the Ramayana. *The whole temple structure is a representation of Shiva's Himalayan home, Kailasa.*

leaf, floating on primeval waters sucking his toe – a symbol of eternity.

PURUSHA, THE COSMIC PERSON

One fascinating creation myth involves the sacrifice of Purusha, the cosmic person. The description of the sacrifice evokes the ritualistic atmosphere of the worship, and the way in which the body of the victim is divided up is said to be the origin of the caste system. This is a translation of some of the verses of the "Hymn to the Cosmic Person." It is part of the *Rig Veda*, the earliest book of the songs

of the ancient seers, which was composed by the Vedic Aryans who came into India from central Asia. They overran the already established Indus Valley civilization. The Vedic period spans approximately 2500 to 600 B.C.

One of the last hymns of the *Rig Veda*, this myth pursues the ancient idea of dismemberment leading to the creation of new life. Purusha, the giant creator being, has a thousand heads, a thousand hands, and a thousand feet. He is the immortal ruler past, present, and future, who pervades everything. The great gods seamlessly arise from him and in turn dismember him and consign him to the funeral pyre. From his mouth, arms, thighs, and feet emerge the four castes, or *varnas,* of Vedic society:

The Moon from his mind was born, and
    from his eyes the Sun.
From his mouth came Indra and Agni,

From his breath was Vayu born.

INDRA AND THE DRAGON
Indra is the most prominent god in the *Rig Veda*. He is identified with thunder and wields the *vajra,* or thunderbolt; his most significant act is the slaying of the dragon Vritra, who

Below: The Orissan builders of Konarak began carving a giant chariot-shaped temple in honor of the Sun god Surya, although the work was abandoned before its completion.

Right: A stone relief showing worshipers circumambulating a stupa. The ritual was performed by entering the east gate and walking clockwise, symbolically following the course of the Sun and putting the worshiper in touch with the cosmos and the spiritual world.

Below:The smooth, rounded forms of these voluptuous figures in the Ramesvara caves are bathed in shadows and diffused light, which accentuates their shapes.

holds captive the Sun and the rain. This deed can be seen to represent either the conquest of India by Aryan warriors, led by their champion, Indra, or as the cosmological allegory of the victory of order over chaos, and the release of the life-giving forces of water, heat, and light.

The seven rivers of the Earth had been swallowed by the evil dragon Vritra and imprisoned in his mountains. Vritra lay down on top of the mountain to guard them, and gradually the land became dry and arid. Without water, the trees and plants began to shrivel and die. Unable to irrigate their crops, the people prayed to the gods to help them, but none of the gods felt strong enough to challenge Vritra. Eventually all the food was used up and the people began to starve, much to the dismay of the gods, who saw that they were powerless to help.

However, Indra, the youngest, yet the most strong-willed of the deities, was determined to do something. He drank three bowls of the magical *soma*, feeling himself becoming stronger with each bowlful. When they were finished, he knew he was mightier than any of the gods, and bravely grasped his thunderbolt, and set out to confront the dragon.

THE DEATH OF VRITRA

When Vritra saw Indra approaching, he let loose the full panoply of his evil powers, trying to overpower the god with blackening fog, blinding lightning, deafening thunder, and piercing hailstones. Indra was impervious to Vritra's earth-shattering attack, and hurled his thunderbolt at Vritra, who fell lifeless to the foot of the mountain. When Vritra's mother appeared to avenge her son, Indra killed her too.

Indra broke open the mountain to free the seven rivers, which poured down the mountain, filling the cracked river beds and reviving the plants, trees, and crops.

THE FIRE OF CREATION

Agni is second only to Indra in the Vedic pantheon of gods. He is the personification and the deification of fire. His three forms are terrestrial as fire, atmospheric as lightning, and celestial as the Sun. He is a messenger between mortals and the gods and therefore particularly important as the sacrificial fire which devours the bodies of the dead.

A thousand headed is the cosmic person.
With a thousand eyes and feet,
Enveloping the earth on all sides,
And going ten fingers beyond.

When they divided the cosmic person,
Into how many parts did they divide him?
What did they call his mouth?

Right: An 11th-century bronze of Agni, the Vedic god of fire, and the link between Heaven and Earth, mortals and gods.

What his arms?
What did they call his legs? What his feet?
His mouth was the priestly class,
His arms the warrior-princes.
His legs were the producers,
His feet the servant class.

From his navel came the atmosphere,
The sky came from his head.
From his feet came Earth, from his ears the
     four regions.
Thus they formed the worlds.
(John M. Koller, *The Indian Way.*)

THE CHURNING OF THE OCEAN

Many cultures used myths to explain natural
phenomena. This ancient myth, originally in
the *Vedas*, not only recounts a classic tale of
good versus evil, but also explains the wax-
ing and waning of the Moon.

    The gods (*Devas*) sought eternal life, and
Vishnu suggested producing an elixir by throwing sacred herbs and precious jewels into the
sea, which they would stir to produce the elixir
of immortality. They uprooted Mount Mandara
and balanced it on the back of a submerged
tortoise to create a paddle to stir the seas, and
wrapped the snake Vasuki around the mountain to create a handle. With his head protruding
at one end and his tail at the other, Vasuki was
pushed and pulled by the gods, who thought
they should be able to rotate the paddle.

    It took all their strength to pull at one end,
so the *Devas* were forced to ask the *Asuras*,

*Right: Sections of a frieze showing the birth
of Buddha; in the center is Queen Maya,
clutching the tree above her. On the right of
the picture are her aristocratic female
attendants. Catching the sacred baby is the
god Indra, and next to him is Brahma.*

or antigods, to pull on the other end, in exchange for a sip of the elixir. This rare moment of cooperation between the forces of good and evil spun the paddle back and forth, creating such friction that the trees on the mountain caught fire, but Indra put them out with his rain.

Having churned the oceans for a hundred years, and after producing the Sun and Moon, several gods and goddesses emerged. First was Lakshmi, who rose from a lotus flower floating on rippling waves. The divine physician eventually held the elixir of eternal life. Immediately, the evil *Asuras* grabbed the elixir before the *Devas* could reach it, but Vishnu distracted the *Asuras* by assuming the form of a beautiful woman, allowing the *Devas* to regain their elixir.

THE BEHEADING OF RAHU

Rahu, one of the *Asuras*, succeeded in snatching a sip of the elixir, but just as he was on the verge of swallowing it, Vishnu beheaded him. Rahu, however, had tasted the elixir of eternal life and could not die, but Vishnu placed his head in the heavens, where it still chases the Sun and Moon. The waning of the Moon is forever associated with the elixir disappearing down Rahu's throat, and then reappearing, causing the Moon to wax once more. When Rahu eventually catches up with the Sun on his eternal chase, he swallows it, causing an eclipse.

Left: A 13th-century sculpture of the Hindu goddess Durga killing the buffalo demon, Mahisha. In her eight arms she carries weapons lent to her by the gods.

Right: An 18th-century Mogul miniature entitled Lovers on a Terrace.

MEASURING THE COSMOS

The key to Hindu cosmology, which introduces the cyclical theory of time and the theory of the transmigration of souls, is the myth of the four ages of humanking.

The four ages, or *Yugas*, are named after four throws of the dice. The *Krita Yuga* was the perfect age, when there were no gods or demons: people were saintly and there was no disease. Sacrifices began during the *Treta Yuga*, when virtue lessened by a quarter. The *Dwapara Yuga* was a decadent age, when virtue lessened by one-half and there came desire, disease, and calamities. And the *Kali Yuga* is the degenerate age, when only one-quarter of virtue remains and people are wicked. The latter is, of course, the age that we live in.

The ancient mathematicians worked out that these four ages spread over 4,320,000 years, and that 1000 of these periods equals one day of Brahma. At the end of each "day" (*kalpa*), Brahma sleeps for a night of equal length, and before he falls asleep the universe is destroyed by fire and flood and becomes as it was in the beginning. He creates anew when he wakes the next morning. A year of Brahma is 360 *kalpas*, and he endures for 100 years – and that is half of his existence. After another 100 years of chaos and disorder, a new Brahma will arise to create a new universe, and so the cycle will begin again.

Left: A miniature of a staged elephant fight, part of the palace entertainment for the Raja of Bundi, seen looking down from the parapet of the Taragarah Fort.

Right: A serene seated Buddha in the Dharmachakra *attitude. This magnificent sculpture in the Gandhara style dates from the 1st century* A.D.

Above: The conception of Buddha. This sculpture shows Queen Maya's dream of the white elephant which circled her three times and then entered her womb. Astrologers predicted that the queen would bear a son destined to become a holy man.

JAIN CREATION

This eternal cycle of creation and destruction is the backdrop to the eternal cycle of birth and death that those who believe in reincarnation must endure. The atheistic Jains reject the doctrines of a divine creator. For them, natural laws provide a more satisfactory explanation. They believe that the world is not created, but is without beginning or end, existing under the compulsion of its own nature. Belief in a creator is considered an evil doctrine and makes no sense, because "If he were transcendent he would not create, for he would be free; nor if involved in transmigration, for then he would not be almighty." (*Sources of Indian Tradition,* ed. T. de Bary.)

Liberation of the soul to eternal bliss requires a detachment from worldly existence. Although the great ascetic philosophy of Jainism rejected much of Hindu thought, the two beliefs shared one vision of the cosmos. The emphasis that Jains laid on wisdom and teaching led to the preservation and creation of many important learned texts on mathematics and other subjects, and also formed a body of popular literature in many different Indian languages. Jain monks devoted a great deal of effort to understanding the cosmography of the universe, and this resulted in the production of many beautiful, highly detailed, illuminated maps. They are revered by Jains and remind them of the extreme importance of making good use of the precious gift of human birth.

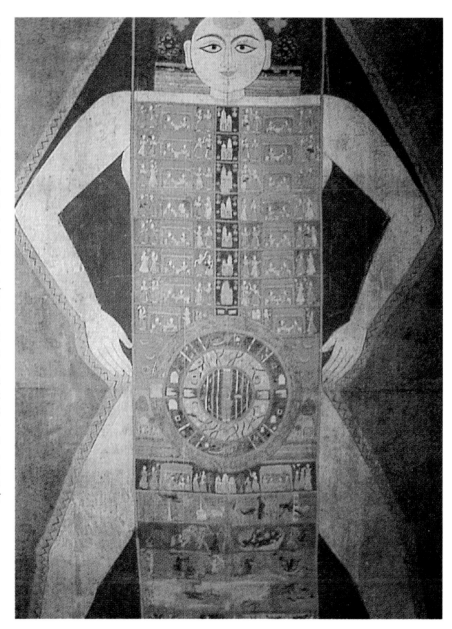

Right: A 17th-century Jain painting of the world in the form of the cosmic man. The middle world is at his navel. Below it are the levels of Hell, and above it the levels of the Heavens.

THE SPREAD OF BUDDHISM

Buddhism, which began in India, has evolved according to national cultures to a bewildering extent. The Zen Buddhism of Japan, the Lamaistic Buddhism of Tibet, and Burmese and Sri Lankan Buddhism all have different emphases, Buddhist sects having quickly sprung up after the 5th century B.C., basing their philosophies upon specific scriptures. Thus Zen Buddhism is based upon meditation in order to achieve "sudden enlightenment," while Tibetan Buddhism, which arrived in Tibet and flourished in the 7th century A.D., emphasizes the practices of the Tantra.

Buddhism is divided into two main schools: the *Theravada,* or *Hinayana,* which predominates in Sri Lanka, Burma, and southeast Asia, and the *Mahayana,* found in China, Korea, and Japan. A chief distinction is the *Mahayana* veneration of the bodhisattva, a person who refuses to enter Nirvana and escape the cycle of death and rebirth – even though he has earned the right – until all the others have been similarly enlightened and saved.

Left: The head of a golden Buddha statue from Thailand. Statues of Buddha all have distinctive historical and regional characteristics.and attributes.

GODS AND GODDESSES

Above: Krishna is Vishnu's eighth incarnation and the representative of personal human love. Here he is seen with Radha, the head gopi *and his consort.*

Previous page: The Khajuraho Temple friezes are some of the world's most exotic and sensual. These carvings date from 1002 A.D.

All Hindu gods and goddesses reside in their own particular place in Heaven, and are worshiped at sacred places of pilgrimage throughout India. A Hindu often adopts a god as his own particular deity, or *ishta-devata,* offering him or her special prayers and worship (although not entirely to the exclusion of other gods). The higher gods of Brahminical Hinduism are called *deva,* the goddesses termed *devi,* and more minor deities and spirits are *devata.* Local or village gods are referred to as the *grama-devata.*

There are innumerable Hindu gods; the *Rig Veda* refers to the fact that there are 33 gods, but then goes on to mention many more by name. Some scholars believe that this means that there are 33 kinds of god. It is probably most simple to say that the Hindus have one divinity which is worshiped in many different guises and aspects.

Brahma, Shiva, and Vishnu are the three most important of the gods. Brahma, the

creator, is not worshiped as a personal god today and there is only one temple dedicated to him in the whole of India. his wife is Sarasvati, the goddess of learning and the patroness of arts, sciences, and speech. Her Earthly embodiment is the River Sarasvati, and as the river she presides over religious festivals and gives fertility and wisdom to the Earth. She may be portrayed holding the stringed instrument, the *vina*, a lotus bud, a book, a rosary, a drum, or a stick of sugar cane.

SHIVA
Shiva is a very ancient god. He is still extremely popular today and is often worshiped in the form of a *lingam*, a stone phallus. He represents the underlying unity of existence in which all opposites are reconciled. He is creator and destroyer. As Lord of the Dance he dances out the awesome rhythms of creation and destruction, but as well as being a

bringer of death, he conquers death and disease and is invoked to cure sickness. He is the great ascetic who has conquered desire, smeared with ashes and haunting the cremation grounds. But at the same time he is erotic, the great lover and passionate husband.

THE MOTHER GODDESS
Shiva's bride is a perfect wife in the forms of Sati and Parvati, but, like Shiva, she also has her horrible forms. As Durga she is the beautiful and ferocious warrior goddess, and as the hideous personification of death and destruction she is Kali, the black earth mother. As Kali, she is usually depicted naked save for a girdle of giant's heads suspended from her waist. She has long, flowing hair and a long necklace of giant's skulls around her neck. Like Shiva, she has a flaming third eye on her forehead. She is usually depicted with four arms: in one she holds a weapon, and in another the

Above: Kanchipuram is one of the seven sacred cities in India and among the most spectacular. The temple complexes are still very much a part of the thriving town, and are not merely archeological curiosities.

Right: A 7th- to 8th-century stone Shiva icon in the form of a lingam, *symbolizing divine power. The face carved on it represents the indwelling deity. A* lingam *occupies a sacred spot in all temples dedicated to Shiva.*

dripping head of a giant; two empty hands are raised to bless her worshipers. She is covered by a tiger skin, and her long tongue protrudes, thirsty for blood. To her devotees, Kali appears as a divine and loving mother who reveals to them the reality of mortality. She not only destroys demons, but also death itself. She appeals especially to those who find the mother-child relationship and symbol more satisfying as a revelation of divine truths:

DUAL NATURES

To the philosopher, these opposing qualities are a paradox, but to the worshiper they represent the richness of existence and the totality of the divine being. The ultimate reconciliation of the conflicts embodied by Shiva is brought about when half his body becomes female and half of him remains male. There are many stories about Shiva and his exploits. In the next one he safeguards immortality.

SHIVA'S BLUE THROAT

Following the advice of Vishnu, the gods and the demons were churning the celestial ocean of milk to obtain from it the nectar of immortality. For a churning rope they used the divine serpent Vasuki, and the great mountain Mandara was the churning rod. They churned furiously for 100 years. Among the first gifts of the celestial ocean were the beautiful goddess Lakshmi, who rose from a lotus flower floating on the rippling waves, and the

Left: An 18th-century image of the divine couple, Shiva and Parvati, with their children at the burning ground; behind them is Shiva's mount, the bull Nandi. Shiva's son, the elephant-headed Ganesh, helps him to make a necklace of skulls. Parvati holds the six-headed son Karttikeya.

divine cow Surabhi, whose son Nandi, the snow-white bull, later became Shiva's companion and mount. The next gift was a crescent Moon, which Shiva snatched from the waves and put on his forehead. Suddenly a terrible, poisonous venom began gushing from the serpent's 1000 mouths, threatening all existence. Moved by the request of the great Vishnu, Shiva swallowed the poison as if it were the nectar of immortality, and saved existence from extermination. The serpent's poison was harmless to the great Shiva, but the venom stained his throat dark blue.

IMAGES OF SHIVA

In painting, Shiva is frequently portrayed with a blue throat and has acquired the epithet *Nilakantha*, or "Blue Throat." A popular image of Shiva is that of "Lord of the Dance," and he is frequently surrounded by a ring of sacred fire. This spectacular icon represents his five divine functions: creation, preservation, destruction, revelation (of ignorance), and release (from rebirth).

But Shiva is most often worshiped as the *lingam*. The *lingam* is usually a cylinder of dark, shiny stone with a curved top set in a circular receptacle, or *yoni,* the symbol of female sexuality. Sometimes there are carvings of the five heads of Shiva on the *lingam*. It represents not only sexuality and the male creative force, but also chastity, as the seed is contained and controlled by yogic meditations. Mythology thrives on such paradoxes, and there are many stories of the conflicts and struggles of Shiva as the erotic ascetic, and of the problems of his unconventional married life.

SATI

This tale tells of the rivalry between Shiva

Above: A 10th-century Chola bronze statue of Shiva Nataraja, Lord of the Dance, from Madras. This is one of the most famous Hindu icons and records the legend of Shiva subjugating 10,000 heretical holy men who had sent a tiger against him. The ring of sacred fire around Shiva represents both the cosmos and the release from Samsara, the cycle of reincarnation.

Right: A 17th-century illustration of Vishnu, worshiped in five manifestations.

Far left: Vishnu, the most popular Hindu deity, and his consort Lakshmi ride on the divine eagle, Garuda. Garuda has symbolic links with the Sun and the sky and derives from a mythical horse named Tarksya. His flight across the sky also represents the Sun's passage during the day.

Left: Krishna subdues the snake demon by dancing on its head in this fragment from a 19th-century Madras temple painting.

and Daksha, the father of his wife Sati. It is with reference to this story that the name Sati is given to the horrendous practice of throwing a widow on her husband's funeral pyre, imbuing what is an act of social and economic expediency with ritual significance.

Right: This miniature, dating from c. 1780, shows Vishnu in his tenth and future incarnation as the white horse, Kalkin.

VISHNU

Vishnu is the most widely worshiped of the Hindu gods. He is all-pervading, the preserver of the world, and his function is to ensure the triumph of good against evil. To this end he often comes to Earth in different incarnations.

The most famous are his lives as the epic heroes Krishna and Rama, but he also appeared as the fish, the tortoise, the boar, the manlion, the dwarf, Parashurama, Buddha, and will come in future as Kalkin.

These incarnations show how Hinduism has

successfully taken over and absorbed popular folk deities (as well as great ones, like Buddha) and the tales associated with them.

Vishnu is often depicted with four arms. He holds in his hands the characteristics symbols of the wheel (the powers of creation and destruction), the conch shell (associated with the origin of existence because of its spiral form, its sound, and its connection with water), and the club (authority or the power of knowledge), and his fourth hand has an upraised palm, expressing reassurance.

LAKSHMI

Vishnu's consort in all his incarnations is Lakshmi, the popular goddess of wealth and good fortune. She is also known as the fickle one, as she is a wanderer who never stays long with anyone. During the festival of Diwali in the late fall, thousands of tiny lanterns are lit all over India, houses are cleaned and decorated until they too are sparkling, and fireworks are let off. All this is to please Lakshmi, who is wandering from house to house looking for somewhere to spend the night and blessing with prosperity all those houses that are well lit.

VISHNU, THE PRESERVER

In his incarnation as the fish, Matsya, Vishnu saved Manu (the father of the world) from a great flood so that his descendants could people the Earth.

While bathing in the river one day, Manu found a tiny fish. The fish begged him to rescue him from the other big fish who wanted to eat him. Manu scooped up the little fish and took him home in an earthenware pot. But Matsya, the fish, soon grew too big for the pot and Manu dug a pond for him to live in. When Matsya had grown too big for the pond he asked Manu to take him to the ocean and release him. As Manu tossed Matsya into the ocean, the fish turned and spoke to him. He warned Manu that in a year's time there would be a great flood, and told him to build a ship to save himself as the whole world would be submerged. Manu did as Matsya had told him, and when the flood came he took refuge in

Left: A stone sculpture of Vishnu in his fourth incarnation as Narasimha, the creature that was half-lion, half-man.

his ship, praising Matsya for saving him.

As the storms grew fierce and dangerous, Matsya appeared again. Now an enormous fish with golden scales and a horn, he attached the ship's cable to his horn and towed it along. Pulling the ship behind him, Matsya swam for many years until they reached Mount Hemavat, the top of which was still above the water. Manu moored the ship to the mountain to await the end of the flood. Before he left, Matsya announced that he was really Vishnu, the preserver, and had saved Manu from the flood in order that he might create new plants, animals, and people for the world.

THE LORD KRISHNA

Krishna is the most beloved of all the Hindu gods. For his worshipers he embodies divine beauty, joy, and love. The playfulness of the divine child and the charming and tender love of the divine youth draw the devotees into the loving embrace of the supreme god. This is the story of the life of Krishna.

The gods wanted someone to destroy the evil king, Kans of Mathura, so Vishnu resolved to be born as the eighth son of the king's sister, Devaki. King Kans was warned of this scheme, so he imprisoned Devaki and her husband, Vasudev, and killed each of their sons as they were born. But when Krishna was born Vishnu appeared to the couple and told them to exchange their baby son for the new-born daughter of a cowherd couple, Yasodha and Nanda, who lived in the village of Gokul across the River Yamuna.

Left: Vishnu as the boar Varaha, lifting the earth goddess from the primeval ocean. In this incarnation he also destroyed the demon Hiranyaksha. This is a Punjab 12th-century stone icon in the Chaunan style.

KRISHNA'S EARLY POWERS

Vasudev found that the doors of the prison were miraculously open and set off for Gokul with the child. He had to cross the River Yamuna in a terrible storm and feared for their safety. The baby Krishna touched the water with his foot and the waves parted, letting them through. Vasudev left the baby with Yasodha, who brought him up as her own son, and returned to jail with the baby girl, who was no threat to King Kans. However, the king found out that Krishna had been saved and sent a demon nurse called Patoona to destroy him. The demon managed to deceive Yasodha and Nanda, but when she gave her breast to the baby Krishna he sucked and sucked until he had sucked all of Patoona's life away.

KRISHNA'S CHILDHOOD

As a child, Krishna was playful and mischievous. Innocent and obedient in his mother's presence, he missed no opportunity for mischief when her back was turned. He untied the village calves and pulled their tails, mocked and laughed at his elders, and teased little babies until they cried, urinated in neighbors' houses, and stole butter and sweets. But Yasodha and Nanda, who had no control over him, just laughed at his antics.

KRISHNA AND KALIYA

When Krishna was about 12, he slew Kaliya, the five-headed serpent king who had been killing chickens, goats, and cattle. He also destroyed the demon Trinavarta, who was sent by King Kans disguised as a whirlwind. As a youth, Krishna enchanted and intoxicated the

Right: A carving of Vishnu as the fish Matsya. As Matsya, Vishnu saved Manu from the great flood.

Right: A highly stylized portrait of Radha, the cowherd woman loved by Krishna. The 18th-century painter, Nihal Chand, is thought to have derived this style from the poetry of his patron, Raja Savant Singh, describing his own beloved, whose nose was "curved and sharp like the thrusting saru cypress plant."

Far right: Gopis *(cowherds)* begging Krishna to return their clothes, which he stole while they were bathing.

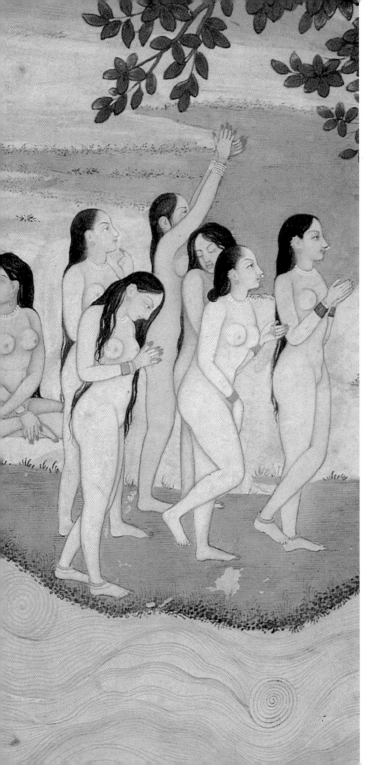

cowherd women with his flute-playing. He teased them and made love to them. His favorite was the beautiful Radha, who took many risks to meet her dark lover:

> How can I describe his relentless flute,
> which pulls virtuous women from their
>> homes
> and drags them by their hair to Krishna
> as thirst and hunger pull the doe to the snare?
>
> Chaste ladies forget their lords,
> wise men forget their wisdom,
> and clinging vines shake loose from their
>> trees
> hearing that music.

(David R. Kinsley, *The Sword and the Flute.*)

THE WRESTLING CONTEST

Eventually stories of Krishna's exploits reached King Kans, and he resolved to try and kill him again. The king announced a wrestling match, and challenged the local young men to try and beat the court champions. His plan was to lure Krishna and his brother, Balaram, into the city and, pretending that it was an accident, release a wild elephant in their path. He felt sure that they would not survive such an encounter.

Krishna and Balaram seized the chance to show off their prowess at wrestling and came to the city on the day of the festivities. When their turn came, they entered the ring to be faced by a wild elephant charging toward them, trumpeting in fury. Without hesitating, Krishna leapt upon the elephant, and, putting his mighty arms around its neck, he squeezed until the creature fell beneath him dead. The crowd cheered and King Kans, more furious and frightened than ever, sent his fearsome champions into the ring. But they were no match for the brothers. Krishna soon broke the neck of the first, and Balaram squeezed the second in a great bearhug until his heart burst. Then Krishna leapt upon King Kans and flung him against the wall, killing him in front of the assembled crowds. He then freed his parents and his grandfather, who was the rightful king.

Many more exploits and marriages of Krishna are recounted in the epic poem the *Mahabharata*. His story reaches its climax when, disguised as a charioteer, he delivers the great moral lecture of the *Bhagavad Gita* while involved in discussion with Arjuna, the night before a battle. He explains the nature of divinity, saying that "the best of everything in the world is a part of me." Krishna's exploits are regarded as representing the intimacy between the faithful and God, and the *Bhagavad Gita* is one of the most sacred books of modern Hinduism.

Below: The young Krishna striking the cow with his cowherd's flask. His half-brother, Balaram, stands behind him, and the scene takes place under a Bo-tree. (10th-century stone relief carving.)

GREAT LEGENDS

Previous page: An 18th-century stone carving of Buddha's first sermon. He is surrounded by followers and sits upon a cosmic wheel, symbolizing the eternity of existence.

Above: A princess and her attendants celebrating Diwali, the festival of lights, in a palace garden. Note the yogis and yoginis – holy men and women – in the bottom left corner. This c. 1760 Mogul painting is by the artist Hunhar.

Many of the dates of the calendar are marked by an event that celebrates the myths and traditions of the culture. When the new harvest of rice is gathered in the villages of Maharashtra, in western India, the villagers dance around a heap of grain with an image of a deity on top. They play a ritualistic riddle game, one-half of the dancers asking the questions and the other half responding. In this way they build up a familiar story, usually formed from of one of the great epics. Although Indian mythology has extremely ancient roots, it still punctuates the rhythms of everyday life and is very much alive today.

Above: A garland-seller in Old Delhi. The number of religious festivals celebrated in India is so great that he is kept busy throughout the year. Possibly the most popular is Dussehra, *which occurs on the tenth day of the rising Moon between September and October and commemorates Rama's great victory over the Demon king, Ravana.*

The legends concerning the lives of the great Hindu deities are collected in the *Puranas,* which explain much of the complex symbolism behind each god. Many of the gods' cults were inspired by these legends.

THE DEATH OF SATI
Daksha was holding a grand sacrifice to which all the gods were invited except Shiva. Sati was furious, but decided to go since it was her own father's house. Shiva was pleased at

her loyalty and fervor, but warned her to be strong. "Daksha will insult me and if you are unable to tolerate his insults, I fear you may come to harm," he said. Sati arrived at the sacrifice and told her father, "My lord is deep in meditation, I come alone." Daksha laughed, seeing his chance to heap insults on his great rival. "It is a disgrace for a god to wear filthy rags, to adorn himself with snakes, and to dance like a madman. I could never understand how a daughter of mine could wish for a creature like that for a husband."

A FIERY END

Trembling with rage, Sati denounced her father before the assembled gods. Since Shiva had instructed her not to take revenge, she immolated herself on the sacrificial fire. Shiva's rage and torment at the loss of his wife created a fearful demon who destroyed everyone who had been at the ceremony. Only when Vishnu interceded did Shiva relent and bring them all back to life. Daksha finally acknowledged that Shiva was a greater god than he, and, as a sign of his foolishness, he wore the head of a goat. Shiva fell into a profound meditation, waiting for the time when his beloved would be reincarnated as Parvati and be his wife again.

THE LORD OF THE DANCE

Shiva is frequently depicted as the Lord of the Dance, a tradition that has its roots in southern India, where the Tamil people used dance to promote the growth of crops. Shiva's dance is entirely consistent with his ancient

Left: An ithyphallic sculpture of Shiva in his creative aspect. The double (or even triple) nature of many Hindu gods often puzzles western observers.

role as a fertility god.

The legend associated with the many-limbed image (see page 38) involved the subjugation of 10,000 heretical holy men, who sent a tiger to devour Shiva. Shiva flayed it, however, and used the skin as a cape. A poisonous snake then attacked him, but he simply hung it around his neck as a garland. Next, a black dwarf attacked him with a club, but Shiva held him down with one foot and danced until the dwarf and the holy men acknowledged him as supreme master of the universe. Shiva beats out the rhythm of creation with a drum and the dwarf who is crushed underfoot symbolizes ignorance.

GANESH, THE ELEPHANT-HEADED GOD

One of the children of Shiva and Parvati is Ganesh, the elephant-headed god. He is the general of Shiva's army, the patron of learning, the giver of good fortune, and a popular deity today. At the beginning of books he is invoked by poets, his image is placed on the ground when a new house is built, and he is honored before a journey is begun or any business undertaken. This is the story of how he came to have an elephant's head.

THE BIRTH OF GANESH

Shiva had been away for years and Parvati was bored and lonely. She decided to make herself a baby to play with and fashioned a small, roly-poly boy out of clay. One day, when Parvati was bathing in a pool, she asked her son Ganesh to make sure no one disturbed her. Shiva arrived home at that moment and started to look for Parvati. The boy, not realizing who it

Right: Shiva walking with the sacred bull Nandi (who represents fertility), accompanied by Parvati, his consort.

was, stopped him from going near the pool. Furious at being opposed, Shiva immediately cut off the boy's head with his sword. Parvati's grief knew no bounds, and she screamed and threw herself sobbing on the ground.

To placate her, Shiva sent 1000 goblins, demons, and imps to look for the head of a male child. They searched all night but, finding each baby animal asleep facing his mother, they did not have the heart to cut off his head. Finally, they found a baby elephant who was sleeping with his head turned away from his mother so that his trunk didn't get entangled with hers and to prevent them snuggling close together. Immediately Shiva's goblins removed his head and brought it to him. As he fitted the elephant's head onto his child's body he breathed life into it and waited for Parvati's reaction. To his surprise, she was delighted.

KALI'S DANCE OF DEATH

A demon named Mahisha was ravaging the world. He seemed invincible, because every drop of blood that he spilled came to life and became 1000 more demons ready to battle. He said that he would be "invincible to all enemies except a woman," so the gods summoned Kali and asked her to destroy the monster. Each god gave Kali a weapon, so she was armed with Shiva's trident, Vishnu's *chakra*, and the wind god's bow and arrows.

Leaping into battle, the terrible goddess slayed 1000 demons with her whirling sword. As she killed them she drank their blood, licking up the drops before they could touch the ground and produce more demons. Finally, only the original monster was left, and she consumed him in one gulp.

Beginning her victory dance, she became more and more frenzied and out of control, threatening creation. Fearing that the universe would be destroyed, the gods came to her husband Shiva and begged him to intercede and stop her wild dance of destruction. But she paid no heed even to him, until in desperation he threw himself down before her. She began to dance on his body. Eventually, realizing what she was doing, she at last came out of her trance and stopped dancing. Thus the universe was saved from the ravages of the mad dance of Kali.

HANUMAN, THE MONKEY GOD

Hanuman, the monkey god, is the son of the wind god Vayu and a semidivine female called Anjana, who was married to the monkey Kesari. Apart from Hanuman's epic exploits as the savior of Sita, there are many other legends abut him. Renowned for his almost supernatural physical strength, he is quasidivine, and is able to change his shape at will. His tail was immensely long and extremely strong.

Once his half-brother, Bhima, came to visit Hanuman, who pretended to be gravely ill. He lay on the ground, with his tail across the path. Bhima was proud of his own physical strength and decided to move Hanuman's tail without disturbing his brother. He was unable to lift it, however, let alone shift it, and was suitably humbled by his own weakness, and more than ever impressed by his brother's powers.

Right: A stone icon of Shiva and Parvati. Parvati, daughter of the sacred mountain, the Himalaya, is the most benign of Shiva's consorts, revered for her gentleness and modesty..

Left: Ganesh, the popular, elephant-headed god, is also known as the "Remover of Obstacles." He has a gentle and affectionate nature, and his image is often found over the main entrance of many Indian homes to ward off evil. Symbolically, his round, fat body contains the whole universe, his trunk can remove obstacles, and his four arms represent the castes that divide the world.

RAMA AND RAVANA

Almost every day of the year somewhere in India a festival is held. At the most popular festivals thousands of people gather to listen to stories of their favorite heroes and gods. Rama is the hero of the great epic, the *Ramayana*, and another incarnation of Vishnu, sent to Earth to kill the demon Ravana. At the Rama-lila, held in Delhi in the fall, there are theatrical performances of the great battle between Rama and Ravana. The performance ends with the immolation of a vast paper effigy of Ravana.

Rama's wife, Sita, is considered to be the perfect wife, and her behavior is held up to young girls to emulate. Sita was abducted by the demon king Ravana and carried off to his kingdom of Lanka. A distraught Rama went in search of her, and in the forest he enlisted the help of the monkey god, Hanuman. In this extract Hanuman uses his magic powers to reach Lanka and discovers Sita.

HANUMAN SAVES SITA

Hanuman learned from Sampati, the brother of the king of the vultures, that Sita had been carried off to the distant island of Lanka, a hundred leagues over the southern ocean. Being the son of Vayu, the wind god, Hanuman resolved to use his powers to leap over the

sea. He filled his lungs with sea wind and, with a mighty roar, rushed to the top of a mountain. Assuming a gigantic form, he leaped into the air and sped across the sea like an arrow. But his path through the air was impeded by demons. Surasa opened her enormous jaws to catch him, but he quickly shrunk to the size of a man's thumb and leapt in and out of her gaping mouth before she could close it.

HANUMAN'S POWERS

Next, his shadow was grabbed by the she-dragon Sinhika, who wanted to devour him. But he wounded and killed her and carried her onto the island. Arriving at night, he turned himself into a cat and crept stealthily around the sumptuous palace looking for Sita. Creeping up the jeweled stairways of gold and silver, he came across the women's chamber. The sleeping, perfumed forms seemed like a wreath of lotus blooms awaiting the kiss of the morning Sun. Outside, in a grove of asoka trees, Hanuman at last saw the long-lost Sita.

Guarded by fierce and ugly demons with the heads of dogs and pigs, she was without fear. Although Ravana came daily, threatening her with torture and death if she would not marry him, she rejected him. She would die before she was unfaithful to Rama. Hanuman secretly approached the beautiful, sorrowing Sita and showed her Rama's ring that he was carrying. He offered to bear her away, but her modesty prevented her from touching the body of any man except her husband. Instead she gave him a jewel from her

Left: Kali, the mother goddess, in her destructive and least maternal form. This 9th-century stone icon from Orissa shows her holding a sword and wearing a garland of giants' skulls.

hair and begged him to tell Rama that she had only two months to live if he did not rescue her. Before he left, Hanuman decided to destroy as much of Ravana's kingdom as he could. Turning himself back into a giant monkey, he started to uproot trees and devastate the countryside, but he was taken prisoner by Ravana's son, the mighty Indrajit, who shot him with a magic serpent arrow. As a gesture of defiance, Ravana set fire to Hanuman's tail and sent him back to Rama as an envoy.

But Sita prayed that he would not burn, and Agni, the god of fire, spared him. As he escaped from the kingdom of Lanka, Hanuman managed to accomplish great destruction by setting fire to many mansions with his flaming tail. On his return, Rama was overjoyed that his beloved Sita had been found, and immediately made preparations to go to her rescue as soon as possible.

BUDDHIST MYTHS

The *Jataka* tales are a collection of 550 stories of the former lives of the Buddha. Some of these tales are peculiarly Buddhistic, but others are evidently part of the contemporary folklore, and have been incorporated into Buddhist mythology. They give us a vivid picture of the social life and customs of ancient India. Some of these tales are quite misogynistic: women are often viewed as the source of all treachery, as in this story about a demon – or *Asura* – who used to come and listen to the preaching of the bodhisattva. The story is

Below: A 20th-century depiction of Hanuman, the monkey god, causing mischief among humans. Note the flames he carries (top right). In this story, Hanuman is protected by Agni, the god of fire.

Left: An 11th-century bronze Tamilwork statue of Hanuman, the monkey god.

a moral tale, which warns against hankering after worldly pleasures, although an alternative interpretation might be that it is about the wiliness of women.

"WELCOME, ALL THREE OF YOU"

The *Asura* lived in the forest next to the highway. When he was not catching and devouring unwary travelers, the *Asura* would go and listen to the teaching of the bodhisattva. One day, he devoured the bodyguard of an exceedingly beautiful noblewoman of the area. She was so beautiful that he carried her off to his cave and took her for his wife. He brought her good things to eat: clarified butter, husked rice, fish, flesh, and fresh fruit. He dressed her in rich robes and ornaments. And to keep her safe, he put her in a box which he swallowed, thus guarding her in his belly.

One day, the *Asura* went to the river to bathe. He threw up the box and let the woman out to enjoy herself in the open air while he bathed a little way off. While the *Asura* was away, she saw a magician flying through the air and beckoned him to her. When the magician came to her, she put him into the box, covering him with her own body and wrapping her garments around him. The *Asura* returned and swallowed the box again, not thinking that there was anyone but the woman inside it.

He decided to go and listen to the teaching of the bodhisattva again and, as he approached, the holy man greeted him, saying, "Welcome to all three of you." The *Asura* was curious to know what this meant, as he had come alone to visit the ascetic. The ascetic told him that he was carrying inside his belly not only his wife, but also the magician. Fearing that the magician might rip open his belly to make his escape, the *Asura* threw up the box again and found his wife and the magician in the box, sporting merrily. The demon was so amazed at the bodhisattva's vision – and so thankful that his life had been saved from the sword of the magician – that he let the woman go and praised the wisdom of the holy man:

> O stern ascetic, thy clear vision saw
> How low poor man, a woman's slave may
>   sink;
> As life itself tho' guarded in my maw,
> The wretch did play the wanton, as I think.
> I tended her with care both day and night,
> As forest hermit cherishes a flame,
> And yet she sinned, beyond all sense of right:
> To do with woman needs must end in shame.
> (*Jataka: Stories of Buddha's Former Births*,
> Ed. E. B. Cowell.)

In other *Jataka* tales the Buddha is born as an animal. In one, he is a monkey who lived alone on the river bank. It is comparable to an Aesop's fable where cleverness outwits force. In Indian tales it is often the crocodile or the tiger, the dangerous animals, who are depicted as fools.

THE FOUR VIRTUES

In the middle of the river was an island on which grew many fruit trees bearing mangos, bread-fruit, and other good things to eat. Each day the monkey would go to the island by jumping first onto a large rock that stuck out of the water, using it as a stepping stone to the island. He would eat his fill and then return home every evening by the same route.

Now, there was a crocodile living in the river who was searching for food for his pregnant wife. He determined to catch the monkey by lying in wait for him on the rock.

BUDDHA'S INCARNATION AS A MONKEY
On his way home, the monkey noticed that the rock was rather higher in the river than usual and called out "Hi rock!" three times. There was silence, so the wise monkey called out, "Why don't you speak to me today, friend?" The foolish crocodile, thinking that the monkey was really expecting the rock to answer shouted out, "It's me, the crocodile,

Below left: The monkey is regarded as a symbol of good luck throughout the Far East. Note the swastikas, ancient symbols of good fortune.

Below: A 16th-century bronze of the hero Rama with his bow.

waiting to catch you and eat your heart." The crafty monkey agreed to give himself up, and told the crocodile to open his mouth to catch him when he jumped. As is well known, when crocodiles open their mouths their eyes close.

So while the crocodile could not see him the monkey used him as his stepping stone, leaping onto his back and then onto the bank of the river and home. The crocodile realized how clever the monkey had been and said "Monkey, he that in this world possesses the four virtues overcomes his foes. And you, I think, possess all four." (The four virtues are friendliness, compassion, joy, and equanimity.)

Tales like this provided endless subject matter for the sculptor and painter, particularly

Above: A Buddhist monk at the Labrang Monastery in Xiahe. Monks have always preserved the holy texts of Buddhism.

Opposite: "The Presentation of the Bowls" to Gautama Buddha. A Buddhist monk's begging bowl is a practical manifestation of his vow of poverty.

as no images of the Buddha were made at first, and he was only symbolized by a wheel, his sandals, his stool, or a Bodhi tree. The railings of the great Buddhist stupas at Barhut and Sanchi are teeming with the characters from these familiar tales, each one with a moral.

ISLAMIC TALES

Muslims entered India as early as the year 711, by the same northwestern route as the ancient Aryan conquerors. In the 17th century, the Mogul Empire, famous for its glittering court, ruled almost all of the Indian Subcontinent. Islam and Hinduism are two very different traditions, and Islamic philosophy did not flourish as much on Indian soil as elsewhere. The literature of the Muslim community came more from Persian traditions. But the meeting of the two cultures did bear fruit. For example, there were areas of common ground over discussions of monoism and monotheism, in the traditions of saints, and especially in the mystic and devotional movements of both religions. Examples of a literature that is both Indian and Muslim are the medieval tales of romantic love. This enchanting story is from the 18th-century poet Mir Hasan.

PRINCESS BADR I MUNIR

The beautiful young prince Benazir was captured by a fairy named Marhukh. She allowed him out on a magic carpet each evening on condition that if he lost his heart to another he would tell her. One night on his travels he came across a group of young women by a watercourse. In the center of the group was the 15-year-old Princess Badr I Munir, clothed in fine and delicate fabrics and adorned with pearls and other priceless jewels. When their eyes met they were both smitten with love and swooned. The affair developed, assisted

by Badr I Munir's closest friend, Najm un Nisa, until the fairy discovered it. Furious at being deceived, she imprisoned Benazir at the bottom of a dried-up well in the middle of the desert, guarded by a *jinn*.

When Benazir came no more to their rendezvous, Badr I Munir grew sick with love, and sorrow, and disappointment. She lost her appetite and wandered about distracted. Crying herself to sleep one night, she dreamed of Benazir and saw his plight. Her friend, Najm un Nisa, decided to go in search of him. Disguised as an ascetic and carrying a lute, she set off. The beauty of her playing attracted the attention of Firoz Shah, the handsome son of the king of the *jinns*.

Najm's own beauty shone through her disguise, and captured the prince's heart, so he carried her off to his father's palace. She stayed at court for some time, playing the lute each evening, until the prince was hopelessly in love with her and begged her to marry him. Before she would agree to his proposal she explained her mission to him and asked for his help in finding Benazir. The king of the *jinns* sent fairies to discover his whereabouts and rebuked Mahrukh for forming such an attachment to a human. Finally Benazir was released from his prison and brought to the palace. Firoz Shah had a magic flying throne, and on it he carried Najm un Nisa and Benazir back to the garden of Badr I Munir.

Their reunion was sweet. Their bodies weak from the sorrow of separation, and their eyes red from weeping, they talked long into the night and slept late into the morning. The following day all four of them took all the necessary steps to ensure that they might be married. The weddings were celebrated with great pomp and ceremony, thus fulfiling the heart's desire of all four lovers.

Left: A Mogul painting from Lucknow, 1775, depicting an Indian princely marriage.

INDIAN MYTHOLOGY AND LEGEND

As befits one of the oldest civilizations on Earth, the mythology of the Indian Subcontinent is without parallel in terms of its entertainment, diversity, and richness.

The gods of Hinduism are at once human and superhuman, and there is a feeling of warmth, and even familiarity, toward them. The greatest lesson of the epics is the final triumph of a kind of cosmic justice, or balance. The charisma of the gods ensures that they remain alive, among their devotees, with their cults reinforced by the many festivals of the Hindu calendar. The main festivals are Holi, which celebrates the New Year in March; Diwali, the celebration of Rama's return from exile, when Lakshmi, the goddess of wealth, is invited into the house; and Dusserah, a nine-day annual celebration of the triumph of good over evil.

All the Indian religions have inspired quite extraordinary works of art and architecture, from the vibrant sculptures and carvings of Hindu temples, to the monumental, beatific Buddhas, to the finely wrought miniatures of the Mogul age. It is a cultural heritage beyond compare, and one which is deservedly celebrated throughout the world.

Left: In front of the pavilion where the prince and his new bride lie is a pool of lotus flowers, while on the roof is a peacock, a symbol of the lovers. A pair of love-birds are in the trees in the foreground. This is an 18th-century painting from Guler.